Dedicated to my scintillating parents

Loving wife Sonia

&

My two angels Rose and Joanna

Contents

Acknowledgements

It would be highly inappropriate for me not to mention how thankful I am:

- To mentor, guru and most important of all, a good friend: George Ukkuru.
- To Santhoshkumar Sasindran my friend for exceptional effort in getting the images right.
- To Ramakanth Kotha and Nandakishore Vijayakumar for pitching in at the right time with support and boosting my confidence.
- To all my friends in UST and GTL, my friends from college for being there always whenever I wanted.

And above all to my wife Sonia and family members for the unwavering moral and emotional support.

1

Current Mobile Testing Trends

In the middle of February 2014 Facebook acquired an 8 MB mobile application called WhatsApp for the staggering amount of $ 19 billion. ABI research predicted that by the end of 2013 the mobile app market would be worth $ 27 billion. However, this figure is dynamic as a large number of mobile applications keep hitting the market on a regular basis.

With the growing number of mobile applications, there is a consequential demand for Testers who are equipped to handle mobile applications testing.

So how do Testers get equipped to meet the market demands, both in numbers and readiness to the new technology?

Smartphones and Operating Systems

Let us start with an assumption that a smart phone is a mini-computer in itself.

So in short, it is a computer that you can carry in your pocket and also make calls with.

These smart phones need an Operating System. Let us examine a few popular operating systems.

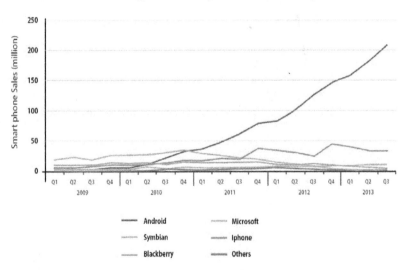

Fig 1 Leading Operating systems

Android

Android is an open source mobile operating system based on the Linux kernel. Android is owned and managed by the Open Handset Alliance - a consortium of hardware, software, and telecommunication companies devoted to advancing open standards for mobile devices. The consortium is led by Google. The latest version in the market is 'Android - 5.0 Lollipop' as this book goes to print.

Based on statistics from the last quarter of 2012, Android has around 70% of market share in terms of mobile operating system. A number of mobile phone hardware manufacturers such as Samsung, LG, HTC and Sony bring out smartphones that run on Android. As Android is open source, most of the manufacturers modify the operating system to suit their hardware. You can access all the Android Smartphone related applications at Google Play stores. You need a valid Gmail ID to access the applications. The extension of the applications that are built for android is (.)APK. Android applications are developed in the Java programming language.

iOS

iOS is a closed source mobile operating system developed and owned by Apple Inc. Most of the handheld devices of Apple such as iPhone, iPod touch, iPad and iPad Mini run on this operating system. Only Apple-made hardware is licensed to run iOS. The current version of iOS is 8.1.2 as this book goes to print.

From the last quarter of 2012, iOS has around 21% of market share in terms of mobile operating system. App Store℠ is the trademark name of the application center for accessing applications that can be installed on iOS phones. Users need to create an Apple ID to download any application from the App Store℠. The extension of the applications that are built for iOS is (.)IPA. As iOS is a closed source operating system, it has a very secure and sturdy architecture. The software required to create iOS applications is called Xcode and is available for free download on Apple computers that run on Mac OS.

Windows Mobile

The mobile operating system that is currently trending is the closed source MS Windows mobile OS developed by Microsoft. Windows mobile runs on smartphones and Pocket PCs. The application center for downloading applications for Windows run smartphones is called Store. Windows phones require a Microsoft account for downloading applications from Store.

A few other trending mobile operating systems:

Firefox OS	Firefox OS	https://www.mozilla.org/en-US/firefox/os/
ubuntu	Ubuntu Mobile	http://www.ubuntu.com/phone
jolla	Jolla	http://jolla.com/
TIZEN	Tizen	https://www.tizen.org/

These operating systems are poised to enter the market with promising features.

The most tedious aspect of building an application for mobile is to ensure coverage of all the operating systems. Each of these operating systems has its own standards, Software Development Kit (SDK) and Application Programming Interface (API) that are compatible only with that specific OS. Hence, as a Tester, one must know the features and specifications of all operating systems before testing the application to ensure complete test coverage, which includes operating system specific Tests.

Check points for testing on different operating systems

The difference in approach between testing a normal desktop / web application on computers and testing a mobile application begins at choosing the operating systems - the base environment of mobile application testing. Consider the following parameters when you test mobile applications:

- **Operating System Major Releases:**
  Operating systems are classified under major releases. These releases are aimed at providing better user experience and features to their users. Let us look at the example of open source OS Android to understand the releases

Alpha	Beta	Cupcake	Donut
Éclair	Froyo	Gingerbread	Honey comb
Ice cream sandwich	Jelly bean	Kit Kat	Lollipop

Each release has increased feature support. For example, the Gingerbread release of Android provided 10 native APIs to help developers build applications. Jelly bean provided 17 APIs. Lollipop, the latest release, has over 5000 APIs.

- **Operating system major version updates**
  Version updates aim at fixing defects and also improving the user experience.
  For example, version 4.0 of a major operating system is released. This operating system, once it enters the market, may get user feedback either in the form of feature usability complaints or defects. When the OS provider makes updates to version 4.0, a version update is released, progressively labeling it as 4.1, 4.2 and so on.

The operating system providers usually inform the developer community in advance about their upcoming releases so that the developers can fine tune their applications to work on the new releases. Testers, however, need to run the entire test cycle on the new build for the new version. So, as a Tester, when you prepare your estimates, consider the time taken for a full round of testing. In the case of OS version updates, Testers also need to consider a few OS version update specific test cases.

- Application behavior on updated OS – Install the application on the existing operating system. Now install the OS updates and continue working on the application. The best approach would be 50-50. That is, run 50% of the existing test cases on this build and the remaining 50% of the test cases in the next scenario.
- Fresh install on the new OS – Delete the existing application and update the OS. Now install the application again on this new environment and test how it behaves. The remaining 50% of the test cases can be executed on this build.

Always use the real device and not simulators for OS migration testing. To get factual and accurate test results, test on real devices. The reasons for this will be discussed in the chapter "Mobile Test tools".

SDK download links:

http://developer.nokia.com/resources/downloads

https://developer.apple.com/xcode/

http://developer.android.com/sdk/index.html

http://developer.blackberry.com/

http://www.microsoft.com/en-us/download/details.aspx?displaylang=en&id=27570

Testing on Tablets

Applications for tablets are also gaining in popularity. The approaches for mobile applications can be used for tablets too. However, mobile web applications that are specific to tablets must be given separate attention right from the beginning. Due to the difference in screen size, web applications have visible changes when loaded in a tablet. Test cases must be fine-tuned to accommodate these changes.

Once detailed testing has been done on a mobile device, testing the same application on tablets should be easier to manage. In most cases the same test cases can be reused for testing on tablets. Follow the same approach described in this book while testing applications on tablets.

Chapter

2

Types of Mobile Applications

As discussed in Chapter 1, users have a number of operating systems to choose from. Hence, applications also need to be built based on the user requirements and the operating system. Analysis from Ads-digital shows that in the year 2012 alone, 46 billion applications were downloaded. It is also predicted that the numbers are going to double each year.

Mobile applications are built for varied reasons such as:

- Improving business by reaching out through hand held devices
- Making it easy to communicate to large groups
- Providing regular and instant updates to customers

The most important reason is that it provides the ability to share updates through multiple platforms. It is about expanding the brand and selling products effectively. For enterprise groups, mobile applications help by keeping the top team always connected and accessible. This helps in handling requests quickly. Most of the Fortune 100 companies agree that mobile applications have helped them to improve customer relations.

Developers can choose between different types of methods for building mobile applications. The types of mobile applications currently available are:

- Native
- Hybrid
- Web
  - Responsive web testing

Native Application

A native application is built for a specific operating system. It will have a home icon, for launching the application by tapping on it. It is very similar to a desktop application. An .exe file can be installed on MS Windows and a .deb file can be installed on an Ubuntu machine. Native apps for iOS devices have an .ipa extension while for Android devices it is .apk. The most important characteristic of a native app is its ability to use all the resources of that device. Resources such as camera, GPS, accelerometer, mic, speaker, Bluetooth etc. can be used to their full potential in a native application by the extensive use of APIs.

Native applications also give users control for offline storage and access to contacts, gallery etc. A native application has the ability to recognize special gestures along with all the standard gestures that the system supports. These applications also get complete control of notifications, which helps in timely alerts and updates to the end user.

Each operating system has a specific Integrated Development Environment (IDE) for building native apps. For building iOS native apps, Apple provides an IDE called Xcode. Android native applications are built using Java. It must be noted that a native application built for a particular OS cannot be installed on another OS. Hence it is tedious to build and maintain. To summarize, in order to build native applications for iOS, Android and Windows, one will have to maintain three separate sets of code created using three different IDEs and test each one separately.

Hybrid Application

Gartner says that by 2016, 50% of the mobile applications deployed will be Hybrid. This is because most enterprises are trying to leverage advanced HTML features and wrap them with native capabilities to create the most useful applications at low cost that are also easy to maintain and share across different OS platforms.

As the name suggests, this type of application is a mix of both native and web capabilities. Just like native applications, they are also distributed through application stores and have a home icon on the device when installed. Hybrid applications have the capability to utilize the hardware of the mobile phones such as camera, GPS, Accelerometer etc. as they are capable of accessing the native APIs. They can also render HTML content from web.

The basic advantage of using a hybrid application is the ease of creating multi OS based applications. The HTML part can be reused in all the applications that are built. Hence the coding effort is reduced when compared with native application development. For companies that cannot afford multiple developers like Objective-C experts for iPhone, Java experts for Android, C# experts for Windows Phone and so on, adapting to Hybrid development can reduce the number of resources required. This helps them create OS specific applications at lower cost.

Some of the leading third party solutions that help build hybrid applications include PhoneGap from Adobe, Titanium from Appcelerator, Apache Cordova and Sencha Touch.

- Cross platform application development:
  As the number of operating systems is increasing, it is important that developers adopt tools that help them build applications for all the leading operating systems with less effort. There are a number of tools currently available in the market that help developers to build applications using a single code base for multiple mobile OS. Some of the leading cross platform application development tools are listed in the table below:

Tool	Link
Xamarin	http://xamarin.com/
PhoneGap	http://phonegap.com/
Appcelerator	http://www.appcelerator.com/
Sencha	http://www.sencha.com/
Qt	http://qt.digia.com/
MoSync	http://www.mosync.com/

As a Tester, it is very important to understand these development tools in order to devise the best test cases. By understanding each of these tools, their pros and cons, one must be able to create test scenarios that ensure the applications work correctly on all expected operating systems. Most of the cross platform development tools have a number of limitations which are exposed only when testing on different devices. In order to bring out these defects hidden in the application it is important to understand the capabilities of the tools used for development.

- Understanding Dalvik and ART in Android
  Dalvik is the virtual machine in the Android operating system that runs the applications. Dalvik uses JIT (Just-In-Time) compilation. This means that the application gets compiled and is ready for running only at the time of its launching. This is a repetitive process that happens every time the application is restarted.
  ART (Android Run Time) is the virtual machine that Google has introduced with its KitKat operating system, which uses AOT (Ahead-of-time) compilation technique. Even though this takes up more time and space initially at the time of application installation, application launching becomes quicker with less processor involvement, which leads to better battery life.
  During testing of Android applications, it would be nice to accommodate the scenarios where the application is tested for both Dalvik and ART runtime options. Even though ART is a new Android runtime, Google is moving away from Dalvik to ART. Hence the applications built must be compatible with both.
  For testing purposes, runtime can be changed on the Android devices by navigating from Settings > Developer Options > Select Runtime
  You will be shown the following screen:

Since ART promises better application speed, it is always good to have the application under test use the ART runtime to ensure it works as expected.

Web

As the title mentions, these are websites specifically crafted to fit into the browsers of smartphones. Of late, due to the advanced and latest features available, HTML5 is widely used for the development of such sites. They do not need to be installed and can be easily accessed from built-in browsers or installed browsers of the smartphone.

Browser details:-

Operating System		Default Browser
iOS		Safari
android		Chrome
		Internet Explorer
		BlackBerry Browser

Some of the other most downloaded free browsers are Opera, Dolphin, Firefox and UC browser.

Even though it is easy to build and maintain, for a Tester the most tedious of all the three (native / hybrid / web) would be to test the web application. One has to test the same web site on different devices, in both landscape and portrait orientation, as web browsers by default support both orientations. One will also need to ensure that web application works as expected in other most downloaded browsers. Hence Testers will end up executing the same test case on the same device multiple times to ensure complete test coverage.

Some of the disadvantages of web applications are:

- They are relatively slow
- Need Internet connection all the time they are running
- Do not have access to device hardware such as camera, GPS etc.
- There is no standard defined, which leads to unpredictable output based on the browser loaded
- There is no app store distribution therefore download and usage statistics are not available

Responsive web testing

The current trend in mobile web application development is building one code based site for all devices. The browser sends the details of the device from which the site is called and the page gets loaded as per the size of the screen. Most mobile sites currently available in the market are created using this technology. There are a number of sites that help to test responsive web behavior. Some of them are:

http://responsivetest.net/
http://mattkersley.com/responsive/

But one important point to be kept in mind while testing using these sites is that they are not substitutes for testing with browsers on actual devices. Always test on browsers that are installed on actual devices to get the exact feel and behavior of the sites. Simulations are not always accurate.

Which one to choose – Native / Hybrid / Web

There is no single answer to this question. The type of application has to be chosen based on the business specific requirement and resources to be utilized.

The following table is created based on the capability of each application type. While this can help as a guide while making a decision, the table can be further expanded taking into consideration other parameters that are apt for the application under test to get the best solution.

Parameters	Native	Hybrid	Web
Cost	✗	?	✓
Maintenance	✗	✗	✓
User Interface	✓	?	?
Platform Independence	✗	?	✓
Speed	✓	?	✗
Installation	?	?	✓
Quick Discoverability	?	?	✓
Device Features	✓	?	✗

 – Best Suited

 – Can be accommodated

 – Not advisable

Chapter

3
Mobile Testing Tools

This chapter discusses the tools that are available in the market for testing mobile applications. The different options available to us for executing mobile testing are:

- Simulators / Emulators
- Cloud Mobile
- Real Device
- Mobile Crowd testing

Simulators / Emulators

These are applications that simulate mobile devices on a computer. Most of the leading device manufacturers create simulators to help developers build applications for the device and test them. Most simulators run on Windows operating system except the iOS simulator, which runs only on Mac OS.

There is some confusion between the terms 'simulator ' and 'emulator '. A Simulator is an application that replicates the software behavior of that device. It gets installed on your computer and uses all the hardware and network resources that are available. Emulators are a bit more advanced; they provide the user with options to set the processer speed, screen size, RAM, Network properties and memory card facilities. Hence an emulator mimics the real device a bit more closely than a simulator does. The best example of a simulator would be the iOS simulator provided in Xcode. And an emulator example would be the Android pack.

Here are the main advantages and disadvantages of simulators / emulators:

Mobile Simulators /Emulators: **PROS**

Cost Factor Mobile emulators are free and provided as part of the SDK with each new OS release.

Simple Just download the software, install on your PC and you're ready to go. Multiple emulators can be run in a simple and straightforward manner.

Fast Since emulators are simple client software that runs locally in your PC, they have less latency than real devices connected to the local network or in the cloud.

Mobile Simulators /Emulators: **CONS**

Increased Risk With emulators, by definition, you are not testing on the same platform and network used by your users. This means that even if all goes well, you cannot be 100% sure that it will actually work on a real device ("false-positives").

Hardware and Software Differences Emulators are typically a "plain vanilla" version of the OS and often do not reflect the specific hardware and software features of each supported device. In addition, as time passes following an OS version release, the emulators are not updated to reflect new devices available in the market.

Different network environment In terms of network configuration, mobile emulators run on the PC (through any personal firewall), connect to the LAN and access the Internet via your corporate firewall. Using real handsets, the network is connected to the radio interface and from there to the Internet. These differences could affect application behavior.

Differences in Computing Resources Depending on the processing power of the PC running the emulator and the type of handset or smartphone being used for testing, performance on the emulator may be unrealistically good or bad.

No way to test network interoperability It is important to test the impact of network-related events (e.g., incoming call, text message, etc.) and different network technologies (e.g., HSPDA, WCDMA, UMTS, LTE) on mobile app behavior. Since emulators are not connected to the mobile network, they do not support interoperability testing.

In short, even though simulators are available freely and are easy to set up, it is not advisable to depend fully on them for testing your application.

Cloud Mobile

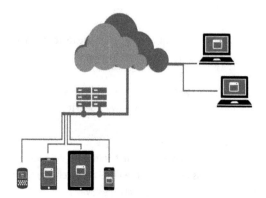

The latest innovation in the mobile development field is the introduction of mobile cloud providers. One of the leading mobile cloud providers, Perfecto, was listed in the top 25 innovations of the year 2013.

One of the myths among users when they hear the word cloud is that they are virtualized. However, mobile cloud providers have nothing to do with virtualization. Most of the leading mobile cloud providers provide access to real devices.

Real devices are connected to a rack that has a facility to support USB connection and uninterrupted power supply. This rack also has a facility to hold a high resolution camera directly above these devices. The cameras capture the screen and are broadcast over the Internet to the end user. The images from the camera are displayed exactly as shown on the device. Now the user can work on these screens using computers, mouse and keyboard. Gestures are captured and transmitted back to the device to carry out the same action on the real device.

Some of the leading providers of cloud mobile are

Device Anywhere: www.keynotedeviceanywhere.com/
Perfecto Mobile: www.perfectomobile.com/
 Some providers like Experitest - http://experitest.com/ even allow you to build your own internal cloud system and share it with remote users.

Cloud mobile providers have a wide range of offers.

- **Public** – This is an open platform where users are allowed to login using a registered ID. Devices are located in the provider's own space at different geographical regions across the world. These devices have different network carriers also enabled on them. This helps the user to understand the behavior of their application on devices that carry different network systems. This also gives us the freedom to test our devices remotely on a variety of devices used in different parts of the world.

- **Private** – These are provided on request. The providers customize the device selection as per the need of the requesters. They also set up the rack with the devices within the requester's space. This gives total control to the customer and also enhanced security, as these devices cannot be accessed by public users.

If you are interested in experimenting hands-on with cloud mobile, you can make use of the free hours provided by the providers listed above while registering at their site.

Cloud mobile has specific advantages and disadvantages. Let us now take a look at some of them:

Advantages of Cloud mobile:
Wide range of devices available: Cloud mobile providers are quick to add new devices to their collection. As soon as a new smart phone is made available in the market, cloud providers get it connected to the existing collection. This helps users to test the application on the latest devices available in the market.

Record videos and capture images: Most cloud providers support recording of the entire test session or part of it. The output video file created is very light in terms of size, which facilitates sharing it with developers to help them in recreating a defect. Sharing the videos with application owners provides an update about the state of testing. The system also allows users to capture images at any point of testing, thus enabling the creation of a meaningful defect report.

Invite other users to a watch or participate in testing: One of the most interesting features of cloud mobile is the option to share the testing device. On selecting 'share' of the device that is opened for testing, the system creates a link which can be shared with anyone connected to the Internet, allowing them to view every action executed on the device in real time. One thing to be noted here is that even users with no cloud provider account can view the testing progress live. They are provided with view only access.

Log files can be extracted easily: Unlike the real device or simulators, the log files of a cloud device can be extracted with one click. This log file also gives the user details of every action triggered on the device. The developer finds it very easy to locate the actual cause of a defect by analyzing this log. The log files play an important role in helping developers fix the defect faster.

Ability to test on multiple networks: One of the most important features provided by cloud providers is the facility to test the application on different networks. They provide Wi-Fi networks and devices connected to different mobile carriers (some of the leading mobile carriers are AT&T, Verizon, and Vodafone etc.). Users need not put in any extra effort to get a device with different network. They can just select the network from the list they are given as soon as they are logged in. This provides the real user experience of the application under test when the selected carrier is used.

Automation capabilities: Most cloud providers have good automation tools in place, which can help the user to automate the application under test without many hurdles. Some providers also help by providing plug-ins, which can be connected to leading automation tools like QTP, to automate the application and run on cloud mobile device. However, lack of consistent standards in coding and timeout issues while executing are still a concern for developers.

Let us now take a look at the disadvantages of using cloud mobile.

Cost factor: Even though users are rapidly provided with the latest smart phones available in the market, the cost factor associated with every license can sometimes be too much for startup companies. Most cloud providers charge annually and the fees may appear onerous for small / medium sized companies. Most mobile cloud providers offer a range of options with a scale of charges.

Slow and not super responsive: As the mobile device is kept in a remote place and actions are triggered from a computer, many factors can affect performance. Most providers use Java UI which is slow and clunky. Users who are familiar with real device testing may experience difficulty adjusting to the change in performance while testing on cloud mobile. The latency of screen refreshing also adds to poor performance.

Touch and gestures aren't that easy to accomplish: Since the actions are triggered at the user's end using a mouse, it is found that many times the results vary. Sometimes when a touch is expected and triggered, the system interprets and executes it as a swipe at the device end resulting in undesired outputs. Some customized gestures cannot be simulated and hence cannot be executed at the device end leading to incomplete testing.

Configuration huddles: Most enterprise applications built these days require a dedicated network to function. Hence it is a tedious job to test such applications on the cloud, as setting up a suitable network is a time consuming business. Because of this, enterprise application testing is often delayed.

Camera use is limited, GPS is always static: As mentioned initially, these cloud mobile devices are kept in a rack at remote facilities. Hence they are always fixed to a particular location.

Therefore, it is not possible to test an application that has mapping capabilities as the device will always give the same location.

Since the camera is also not accessible to the user, testing of applications that require scanning of bar codes or taking a specific picture cannot be executed on a cloud mobile. Some providers have come up with a USB device that acts as a camera for the application so that users can connect this device to the computer on which they are accessing the cloud mobile and send photos from this USB device to the application under test. But this can increase the cost of testing, as additional charges are levied for the USB device.

Data security: Security is a primary concern for enterprises. Many enterprises develop innovative applications which, if leaked to their competitors, could cause catastrophic losses to the company Therefore they go to great lengths to protect their application. In such a scenario, cloud may not be an advisable option. Even though most providers have the 'Wipe Device' option which they claim will reset the mobile to its original factory settings, practical experience has demonstrated that some applications do not get removed.

Apps from other vendors show up: Following on from the above point on security, this is yet another disadvantage of using cloud mobile. Since the device is attached to servers which are accessed by many people, it is possible that the phone could have a number of applications installed, which may affect the device performance. Theoretically it could even enable data theft from another installed application, including the application under testing. This means there is always a security issue associated with applications being tested on devices placed in the public cloud.

Limited access – User based licenses. Only a selected number of users will have access to the device at any point of time. This will be an impediment while trying to load test or even when testing to test on multiple devices simultaneously.

Device offline issues – It takes time to bring back a disconnected device.

Real Device

The best tool for testing mobile applications is the real device itself. It provides the real user experience and also helps identify many defects. However, it is nearly impossible for a company to test on all real devices. Studies in the last quarter of 2013 show that at an average of 6 to 8 smart phones are being introduced into the market every quarter. This number is growing all the time. Most smart phone manufactures like Samsung, LG, HTC, Apple, Nokia and so on are in pursuit of capturing market share by producing new handsets on a regular basis. Unlike the old consumer habit of following success and buying only what is established in the market, users are now ready to check out new devices even without a single review. This has increased the breadth of devices that a Tester has to cover while testing mobile applications.

It follows that for a mobile application Tester, many parameters have to be taken into consideration when procuring devices. Some of them are:

- o Popularity of the device / manufacturer
- o Operating system running on the device
- o Screen resolution
- o Geographical region for which application is built (to consider the leading devices in that area)

Now let us try to understand the advantages and disadvantages of using real devices for mobile application testing.

Advantages:

Reliability - Testing on real handsets always give you accurate results (no false positives or false negatives). Application behavior for all kinds of actions and its interaction with other hardware (camera, accelerometer, GPS etc.) or software (contacts, calendar, gallery, messages etc.) resources of the phone also can be recorded accurately when tested on a real device.

Interoperability testing – Interoperability testing is about assessing the application behavior when there is a switch between networks. Real device testing is typically performed in a live network. Unlike simulators or even cloud mobile, real life interoperability testing like shifting from a Wi-Fi signal to mobile carrier Internet can be reproduced for real and the effects on the application can be assessed correctly.

Some of the interoperability test scenarios are:

- Mobile network to Wi-Fi – Start working on the application from a mobile network and walk into an already paired Wi-Fi connection
- Wi-Fi to mobile network - Start working on the application from a Wi-Fi connected area and walk away while working on the application until the device automatically loses the Wi-Fi signal and connects to mobile network
- 3G to 2G
- 2G to 3G
- No Network – There are two way to test this condition. One is to manually turn on the Airplane mode of the device and another is to take the device into a tightly enclosed area where there is no network available to create a natural network loss.

True user experience - Testing on real devices is the only way to truly understand the user experience, taking into account the CPU, memory, screen size, etc. for a given device. Actual behavior of the application can be correctly judged while testing on real devices. Fonts, font sizes for readability, images for visible defects etc. can be tested correctly on real devices. The best method for testing mobile applications for user experience is on a real device.

Performance testing - It's easier to expose performance defects with real handsets, as well as defects which are the result of the handset itself or its environment. One of the simplest methods to carry out performance testing of mobile applications is by using real devices. The Tester must use a stop watch to calculate the time taken for each action like opening of the application, time taken for flash screen to load, etc. It is also very important to take note of module to module transition time in the first round of testing so that it can help the developers to fine tune their code to avoid any excessive delay in this aspect. Testing on real devices also enables us to identify areas where activity indicators must be introduced to avoid confusion to the end users caused by displaying blank screens when the intended action takes longer than expected to load the result.

Concurrent Testers– Having multiple devices available for testing helps the Tester to test the same application concurrently. This can help in identifying further performance issues associated with the application when used by multiple users.

Automation Testing – Tools like SeeTest give ample opportunity to automate applications. Automating applications using real devices is found to give much better results when compared with the cloud automation method. Users complain of timeout issues while automating using cloud mobile. These disappear when automated using real devices. Also, debugging becomes easier as the device is available at hand. The automation features available for mobile application testing are discussed in the chapter 'Mobile application automation and performance testing'.

Now for some of the disadvantages of real device testing:

Cumbersome for development - In the initial development stages, real handsets are harder to connect to the IDE than emulators. This can slow down the debugging process.

Security issues - If you are using devices connected locally to your workstation, you will need to make sure USB ports are open. In addition, mobile devices can easily be stolen, allowing unauthorized access to internal network resources.

Location Limitation - Since the devices are accessed from offshore centers, one may not get the actual mobile network performance result while testing.

Mobile Crowd testing:

Another very innovative and trending test approach for mobile application testing currently in practice is Mobile Crowd testing. Mobile crowd testing takes its cue from the crowd testing technique which is widely in use for testing websites. Here the Testers are anyone who is an owner of a mobile device. There are many leading mobile crowd testing groups. Some of them are:

- www.utest.com
- www.mob4hire.com
- www.testbirds.com
- https://bugcrowd.com

These sites basically act as an agent between mobile application developer and Testers. Test enthusiasts sign into these sites and obtain regular updates whenever there is an application to test. Users from across the globe download the application and test under different conditions. This helps in identifying many defects in a short time. The test enthusiasts are also rewarded in many ways. Some of the most common reward methods are:

- Rate per test hours
- Rate per bug

This method of testing for mobile applications is really taking off as it allows developers to get a feel for the application in a number of scenarios. Using crowd testing, one gets to check the following parameters that are very relevant to a mobile application:

- Varity of devices
- Varity of Operating Systems and different versions
- Varity of mobile networks
- Wide geographical coverage.

Developers can get good results with less test cycle investment for applications that are intended for consumers and the general public by way of crowd testing.

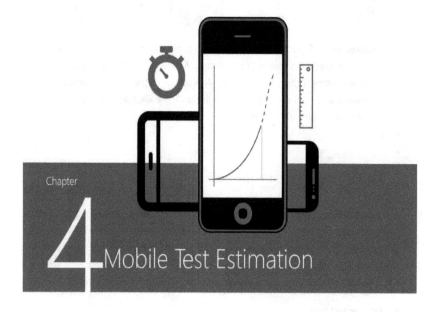

4 Mobile Test Estimation

While normal estimating techniques can be easily applied to mobile testing, it has been found from experience that estimating test effort for mobile applications can be done in a much better and simpler way resulting in greater accuracy and coverage.

It is also good to apply a mobile testing specific checklist to the application beforehand. Some of the check list points that can help you arrive at an accurate estimate are:

- o Application type - Web / Hybrid / Native
- o User coverage - Enterprise / Public
- o Operating systems
- o Operating system versions
- o Orientation - Landscape / Portrait
- o For web applications, details of the browsers it must support
- o For enterprise applications, details of the device list approved by the company
- o Networks - Wi-Fi / 2G / 3G / Combination

Having these questions answered clearly helps in making accurate estimates.

Wire-frames

For a mobile application the best estimate can be reached if the testing team is provided with wire-frames. Wire-frames are step by step pictorial representations of each screen within the application. These days, mobile applications have a set style of development and wire-frames are the basic pillars of this. These representations help users to understand the application and suggest changes at the initial stages. A number of methods are adopted for wire-frame sharing such as jpeg images, pdf, power point presentations and so on. Once there is a well-defined wire-frame in place it will be easy to co-relate it to the requirements and any gaps can be easily captured and rectified.

There are a number of sites and applications that help with the creation of wire-frames. Some applications are so advanced that they can even create responsive application wire-frames which, when fed with dummy data, work exactly like the original application. Many of the leading IT companies are utilizing such wire-frame builders to give the client an exact replica of the actual application at the initial stages.

Some of the leading sites / applications that help with building wire-frames are:

Framer - http://www.framerjs.com/ - A prototyping tool for animation and interaction on desktop and mobile

Indigo Studio - http://www.infragistics.com/products/indigo-studio/ - Storyboarding, Wireframing, and Code-Free Prototyping for Web, Desktop, and Mobile Apps

Mockingbird - https://gomockingbird.com - online tool that makes it easy to create, link together, preview, and share mockups of website or mobile applications.

Simulify - http://simulify.com/ - Interactive and Shareable Wireframes/ Mockups/ Prototypes

Solidify - http://www.solidifyapp.com/ - Solidify helps create clickable prototypes from sketches, wireframe, or mockup

Appery.io - appery.io - cloud-based platform with visual development tools and integrated backend services

Lovely Charts - http://www.lovelycharts.com/ - Lovely Charts is a diagramming application that allows creation of professional looking diagrams of all kinds, such as flowcharts, sitemaps, business processes, organization charts, wireframes

ForeUI - http://www.foreui.com/ - Easy to use UI prototyping tool

Creately - http://creately.com/ - Real-Time collaboration and projects help you work with clients and colleagues

Lumzy - http://www.lumzy.com/ - A functional prototyping tool where user actions can trigger popups, alerts, page navigation, etc.

You can find a number of similar sites / tools on the Internet that help you build wire-frames easily.

An example for a wire-frame of a simple search application can be depicted as shown below

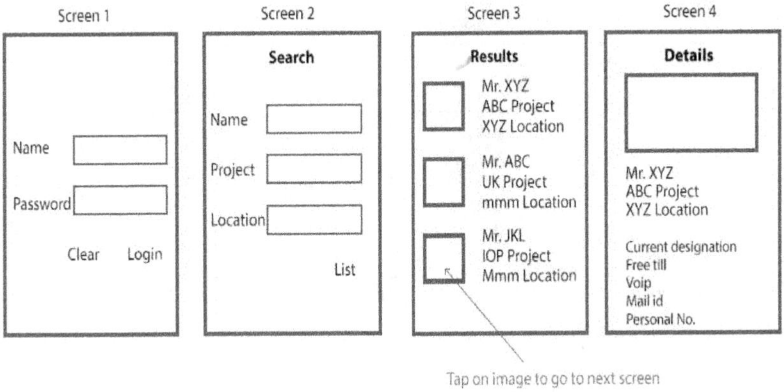

Screen 1	Screen 2	Screen 3	Screen 4

Screen 1

Name [ ]

Password [ ]

Clear   Login

Screen 2

Search

Name [ ]

Project [ ]

Location [ ]

List

Screen 3

Results

[ ] Mr. XYZ
ABC Project
XYZ Location

[ ] Mr. ABC
UK Project
mmm Location

[ ] Mr. JKL
IOP Project
Mmm Location

Tap on image to go to next screen

Screen 4

Details

[   ]

Mr. XYZ
ABC Project
XYZ Location

Current designation
Free till
Voip
Mail id
Personal No.

Testers can do a round of static testing on the wire-frame to ensure that there are no gaps. This static testing should not take more than a working day to yield results. Testers can share the results with the client and engage in a discussion to evaluate each observation. Approved observations must be forwarded to the UI team to ensure the changes are updated in the next version.

Once the approved wire- frame is available, test estimation can be carried out. Testers who are not comfortable with this approach can apply the normal estimation technique of mapping the requirements and its complexity to arrive at the final analysis. However, having worked on more than 100 mobile applications, the author is sure that one can reach a refined accurate estimate using the wire-frame approach.

This example will help in understanding how to do mobile application test estimation.
"A fortune 100 company with 50000 employees needs a web application and wants this application to run only on enterprise devices and must support all native browsers, Firefox and Chrome."

The completed checklist might look like this:

Application type - Web / Hybrid / Native	Web
User coverage - Enterprise / Public	Enterprise
Operating systems	BlackBerry OS , iOS, Android
Operating system versions	BlackBerry Version 6.0 iOS version 7.1 (For both iPhone and iPad) Android 4.2 (KitKat for phone) Android 3.2 (Honeycomb for tab)
Orientation - Landscape / Portrait	Both
For web applications details of the browsers it must support	Default, Chrome, Firefox
For enterprise applications details of the device list approved by the company	iPhone 4 - 3000 Blackberry 9000 - 4000 iPad3 -1000 Samsung galaxy tab 10.1 -1500 Nexus 5 - 500
Networks - Wi-Fi / 2G / 3G / Combination	Wi-Fi and 3G with Corporate connection

The next important step is device selection criteria, which is explained below:

Based on the data in the checklist above it is evident that testing must be restricted to theses five devices:

Device Details			Browser Details		
Device	Operating System	Screen Resolution	Browser 1	Browser 2	Browser 3
iPhone 4	iOS 7.1	960×640	Safari	Chrome	Firefox
Blackberry 9000	Blackberry OS 6	480 x 320	BlackBerry Browser	N/A	N/A
iPad3	iOS 7.1	2048x1536	Safari	Chrome	Firefox
Samsung galaxy tab 10.1	Android 3.2 (Honeycomb)	800 x 1280	Chrome	Firefox	N/A
Nexus 5	Android 4.2 (KitKat)	1080 x 1920	Chrome	Firefox	N/A

	Landscape Orientation			Portrait Orientation		
	Browser 1	Browser 2	Browser 3	Browser 1	Browser 2	Browser 3
	100%	100%	100%	100%	100%	100%
	100%	0%	0%	100%	0%	0%
	100%	100%	100%	100%	100%	100%
	100%	100%	0%	100%	100%	0%
	100%	100%	0%	100%	100%	0%
Cycles	5	4	2	5	4	2

Total number of Cycles - 22

Unlike any other applications testing, be it desktop applications or web applications to be run on computers, what makes mobile application testing special is the above table. The same set of test cases must be executed 22 times just for the small example considered to get the best results. Normally, the mobile applications testing cycle is almost 5 to 6 times greater than the development cycle. That is, for a mobile web application that takes 100 hours to develop, it needs a minimum of 500 to 600 hours of testing just for one round.

The estimation of cycles becomes a tedious job when building an application for public use. Device details obtained in the sample case above may not be easy to obtain for a public case study. Some effort may be required to extract the key elements from data that is readily available online. Many sites like Gartner, Bitpipe, Forrester, to name few, specialize in providing the latest statistics on almost all topics related to emerging trends.

While considering an estimate for an application meant for the public, consider the following factors

- Screen Spread
- Domain spread - phone vs tablet
- Operating System spread
- Popular Phone chart
- Manufacturer spread
- Browser spread

In the example it must be noted that only execution cycles are considered. However, there are many other associated activities, just like any other application, that also must be covered under estimating. Some of them are:

Distribution method

To have a proper testing strategy in place, it is very important to have the distribution method defined initially. This is applicable to native, web and hybrid applications. There are two leading distribution methods:

- Enterprise
- Public

Enterprise

Enterprise distribution is adopted mainly when companies want to restrict the distribution of an application to a particular group. There are also companies that insist on having web applications that work only when the device is connected to their network. For a mobile device, a particular connection can be established either by a VPN token or by using the company Wi-Fi connection. Enterprise applications make estimating easier as they help narrow down the device selection to a controllable size.

Most leading companies use devices only after proper testing and conformance to their own security regulations. Hence the number of devices available to an employee from a company will always be limited. This helps us to prepare an accurate estimate, ensuring coverage on maximum devices allowed by the company.

While testing an enterprise application, Testers have to ensure that the first test case must be to confirm that its working when accessed from a network which is outside the permitted one. A suitable notification must be in place for all such cases. "Your application is currently not available since you are not connected to the company network. Please connect to the company network and try again" is a very meaningful message that can be shown at the application loading time if the user is not connected to the expected network. The same notification must be applied for the web application too.

It is also important while estimating enterprise application test time to add the testing time required for checking the application installation methods. Most companies have in house application distribution systems, which are websites or mobile device management systems (which will be discussed in the chapter entitled 'Mobile Device Management'). This installation testing and its associated activities like actual installation on the device, update and so on, must be estimated to provide greater accuracy for test estimation.

Test estimates for Enterprise mobile applications have more accuracy than for those for the public due to the completeness of the data available.

Public

The toughest part of a mobile application testing estimate is estimating the effort of testing an application that is meant to go public. A number of parameters need to be considered for testing an application that is for the public distribution. Some of them are:

- Devices supported
- Browsers supported
- Networks
- Application distribution channels such as Appstore, AppWorld, Google play etc.

Devices Supported: For a public application, this is the biggest challenge a testing team has to solve. To narrow down the number of devices to be tested on becomes the most tedious job. There are a number of methods that can be used to reduce the number of devices to be tested.

One method is to check the application platform, for which OS application is built for. Once a definite answer is available the next step would be to search for or take the help of leading statistics providers to get the best-selling device list. There are a number of data providers who can be trusted to make this selection. One point to be noted here is that, even though the manufactures are different, if there are several devices with the same screen resolution and operating system only one device needs to be chosen.

Another method is to narrow down using the geographical area. If the application or site to be tested is to be used only in a selected region one must stick to the data from that region to make the selection.

Prepare a table as shown below while searching for the details of the device

Device Manufacturer	Operating system	Operating system version	Screen Resolution

Once the table is filled, the number of devices to be tested can be narrowed down in consultation with the client. The best approach for the sake of preparing an estimate would be to select the top 10 devices from the list. Once it is presented to the client, if they want to accommodate more devices, estimating can be improvised by adding more devices from this list.

Browsers supported: When approaching the estimation of a web application it is very important that the most popular browsers are considered. Most devices have default browsers. However, users might install additional browsers to suit their requirements. Confirmation from the application owner must be obtained on the number of browsers required to support the site under test. Once the data is available it will help to fill this table:

Device	Resolution	Device OS	Browsers

These details can help in building an accurate estimate for the mobile web application under testing.

Networks: Another important parameter that helps us in test estimation is the networks to be supported. In most cases all mobile networks are by default supported. But it is not possible to proceed with this assumption for the estimate as there are a number of applications that work only when connected to Wi-Fi or 3G. Hence the details must be obtained at the initial stage to estimate the test time.

Some of the options are:

- 2G
- 3G
- Wi-Fi

Once the list is ready, be sure to execute all the test cases against each network type to confirm errorless execution of the application under test. From experience it is found that even though some functions work properly when connected to Wi-Fi they may not give the correct results while accessed using a mobile network. Therefore, for an application that is expected to work on mobile network and Wi-Fi, entire test cases must be executed on both connections separately.

Care also must be taken to consider the time required for interoperability (which will be discussed in the chapter 'Actual Mobile Test Execution'). The best approach for interoperability testing would be to narrow down the test cases to those that require data upload or download, and carry out the interoperability testing while executing these test cases.

Application distribution channels such as Appstore, AppWorld, Google play etc.: For a native application that needs to be shared with the public through application distribution systems of leading operating systems, one must ensure thorough testing with test cases covering the guidelines for application development. These guidelines are unique to each leading application store. Adherence is assessed prior to releasing our applications through their channels. Any deviations from the guidelines results in the rejection of that application which again can lead to rework and delay the release date by another 10 or more days. Hence Testers must ensure coverage of application submission guidelines testing in their test cycle and estimates must include this too.

Always have a white-box test cycle put in place to ensure proper data encryption and other checks like testing for transfer of data from the device without the permission of the user etc. before submitting the application for distribution.

Some of the leading Operating system application submission guidelines can be accessed from this table:

Operating system	Owner	Application store	Link
iOS			https://developer.apple.com/app-store/review/
ANDROID			http://developer.android.com/distribute/googleplay/publish/preparing.html
			http://developer.blackberry.com/devzone/blackberryworld/preparing_your_app_for_blackberry_world.html
			https://developer.windowsmobile.com/en-us

Test methods

The method to be applied for mobile application testing needs detailed analysis.

The methods available to test a mobile application are:

- Manual
- Automation
- Cloud
- Crowd

Many factors must be considered before making the final call. Some of the questions that can help you arrive at a proper selection are:

- Approximate budget of the application testing
- Application life cycle – Agile / Normal SDLC
- Duration of application life cycle – Long / Short
- Complexity of the application – Complex / Medium / Normal
- Geographical coverage – Enterprise / Public
- Application connections – Standalone / part of web or desktop application

- Tool availability – Automation tool available that supports mobile application automation / Need to purchase new tool

Once these questions are answered it will help in choosing the right approach for testing a mobile application. All possible approaches are discussed below in detail:

Manual: The preferred method of approaching mobile testing. Since most of the applications that are built for mobile have a short life span, this approach suits best. Manual testing involves less setup costs, as most mobile applications are self-explanatory and do not involve any training. This method also helps to access real time performance of the application. The manual approach is also best suited for applications that follow an agile development cycle as it helps the team build and execute test cases in a very short time span.

A manual testing approach must begin with testing of wireframes and then on simulators before proceeding to testing on actual devices. Wireframe static testing and testing on simulators will help us identify UI/ UX gaps. This will also save time as they are identified at the beginning. Hence it is always advised to have multiple rounds of testing on each tool that is available, to get the maximum benefit.

While estimating for manual testing of a mobile application, it is always good to factor in a number of mandatory cycles:

1. Wire frame testing / static testing
2. Simulator testing of first build to check for UI defects
3. Actual device testing to ensure performance and to avoid functional defects
4. Simulator testing for security

Hence the manual test cycle must consist of at least 4 rounds of testing. Except for actual device testing, for all the other test cycles the time required is much less. Considering all the above points will help you define a proper estimate for manual testing.

Prototyping - Prototyping is yet another feature which has been used extensively by the UI developers for designing mobile applications. Prototyping is nothing but creating a replica of the actual application without interactions with database or network. This is usually a stand-alone program that helps the application owners to understand how the actual application will look. It will be an interactive model that will mimic the original application as regards text boxes, drop downs, swipes, buttons labels etc. These types of interactive wireframes or prototypes are gaining popularity for their simplicity and power to convey the actual look and feel of the application even before a single line of code is written.

Automation: Automation is gathering momentum in the mobile testing space. In the last quarter alone, a number of new tools were introduced into the market to help users automate mobile applications testing. But the decision to automate a mobile application must be taken only after considering a number of factors.

Some of the important factors that you must consider when deciding about automation of a mobile application are:

- o Application life period: This must be the first criterion to be examined when deciding on automating an application. Market research shows that around 60% of mobile applications undergo only a couple of updates and after that they are either abandoned for a better application or simply discarded due to lack of use. Therefore, such an application is not a candidate for automation. So it is important to understand the life period of the application. If the application is going to be around for a really long period and undergoes regular periodic updates, then automation can help reduce the regression test cycle thus helping in faster release of the application.

- o Cost: The next step involved in the automation feasibility study would be to check on the cost factors. One must calculate the cost of automation and check with the application owners to see if they are willing to invest in it. Some of the factors associated with the cost of automation are:

  - Tool cost – The most important factor. Most of the time the cost of purchasing the tool and setting up the necessary environment is a costly affair. Hence while estimating it is good to have an idea of the cost involved in setting up a new tool or, even for that matter, the cost associated with using an existing tool.

  - Training cost – If the tool is new, it may require extra expenditure for resource training or even to recruit experienced resources. This must be foreseen and costed while estimating.

  - Return on investment – If ROI cannot be achieved after eight quarters, then it may be difficult to justify automation costs to the application owners.

- o Resource availability: Estimation also must consider the availability of trained resources. If properly trained resources are not available, action must be initiated to either bring on board sufficiently skilled resources or existing resources must be trained to handle the testing. This becomes all the more important when considering automation. The estimate must also include the time required for training resources if they are new to the tool.

- o Time lines: Most mobile applications have a very limited delivery time and this is predefined even before the first line of code is written. Hence it is very important to have an idea of these timelines so that one can ensure adherence to the delivery date while estimating time for testing. This also helps in figuring out the number of resources and environment (devices, simulator, cloud device etc.) that will be needed in order to meet the expected timelines.

- o Data management: Data management is another important aspect that must be considered well in advance to avoid any delays in the later stages of testing. Test data is spread across the entire testing process right from test planning to test execution. Let us not go in to other aspects but stick to the data management relating to automation here.

  If the application under test is a forked version of any existing web or desktop application, proper data availability for the mobile application must be ensured. All the data requirements must be assessed at the time of wireframe testing. Here the data processing follows different stages of evaluation. It begins with identification of the test data followed by acquisition, conditioning, population of the test data and then maintenance. Estimating must cover all these stages and proper time slots must be allocated for each of them to complete the data management stage.

From each screen, take note of the incoming data for display and input data that will be sent to the server. This data must be made available in the test environment. Any structured data required for testing must be checked with the application owners, to ensure it is available on time for testing to avoid delays. The complexity of acquiring the correct test data must be analyzed at the initial stages to have a proper action in place to ensure data availability on time for testing. Any delays at any stages mentioned above must be accommodated properly in the estimate.

o   Maintenance / Reusability: Ease of maintenance and reusability of the test script must be given utmost priority while planning for automation of an application. If the script created is very complex and reusability is limited, return on investment will take a longer period, which may end up in outdated software usage. Hence to avoid such situations in the planning stage, make sure to analyze the tool and its history of adapting to newer technology.

Reusable scripts must accommodate navigation, data entry and validation, alert management etc. These scripts must be grouped and must be available to be called from anywhere within the entire test script. Reusable scripts are the basic building blocks of successful automation. Hence at the planning stages proper time must be allocated to evaluate the tools capability to create reusable scripts.

Cloud: In order to understand this topic it would be good to take a very close look at the results of the check list that is mentioned at the beginning of this topic to choose the test medium. Cloud mobile testing is costly when considered for a shorter project. Estimation must consider the time required to setup the environment and also time for any specific network connections to be put in place.

Once the setting up of the environment and other associated factors have been estimated, the same method adopted for manual testing can be applied here too. But one point to keep in mind is the delay factor: a normal test case that may take 4 minutes to execute on a real device may take 6 or 7 minutes on the cloud device. This is due to many factors which are already discussed in detail in our previous chapter. In short, Testers must provide at least 10 to 20% buffer time to execute test cases on the cloud.

Crowd: This is the approach most suited for a public application which will give developers actual usage feedback since a large audience is involved. A typical user will be interested in knowing about the application from a normal usability perspective and may even cover scenarios that a Tester would not have considered in their test cases. This can come in very handy for the application owners to collect feedback about the application in the beta testing stages.

Crowd testing has several challenges. One must have a solid user base to which the application can be shared and must ensure active participation of the user group. It is always advisable to have the crowd testing be conducted at a particular time as this will also help the application owners understand the performance of the application when multiple users hit the application at the same time. Estimating for crowd source testing needs detailed planning and also requires a support system to be in place. It can be difficult to maintain the group's interest, which is the major challenge. The active participation of the group can be ensured by putting in place proper rewards and recognition for each valuable defect discovered or enhancement suggested.

When opting for crowd testing, sufficient consideration must be given to the effort required for consolidating the defects or suggestions received from the group and the time required for the defect triage meetings. It would be also good to have a small online session conducted with the prospective Testers to inform them about the application, its uses and the workflow so that they have an opportunity to ask questions before actually using the application. This will help in getting better results.

5 Actual mobile test execution

Now that the basics have been discussed and established, it's time to get our hands dirty with the actual test execution. The point to be noted here is no matter on how many devices one tests, the execution cycle stays the same. Mobile testing is all about repetition and the need to keep executing the same cycle on a number of devices. So it would be nice to build a framework that can be applied to all cases.

This chapter elaborates on the major check points that must be covered in the actual mobile testing. A junior Tester or anyone interested in learning the basics of mobile testing can refer this chapter to begin working. It explains the major areas that one must consider and cover while testing a mobile application.

 Nonfunctional: Any action on the device that is not connected with the application under testing can be termed as a non-functional requirement. The non-functional requirement plays a very important role in mobile applications. It consists of a common set of cases that must be considered for every mobile application under test.

Some of the most common non-functional areas that a mobile Tester must consider while creating a checklist are:

- Usability
- Accessibility
- Security
- Performance
- Localization
- Stability
- Device hardware behavior

To give an example, a non-functional test can be to switch from the application under test and open the camera and click a random photo. Now go back to the application under test to see if this interruption has any effect on the application.

To avoid confusion let us try to understand the difference between a functional requirement and a non-functional requirement. For a mobile application that has a log in screen, a functional requirement could be "Application must have a login screen". Now to extract the non-functional requirement from this statement would be like "The logging in time must be less than 6 seconds." So in this manner, one must be able to list a number of non-functional requirements associated with every functional requirement the application has. Also there are many non-functional requirements that can be considered from the device standalone perspective.

It is always advisable to have a detailed checklist prepared to cover all the non-functional aspects of a mobile application. This checklist must be created keeping in mind its reusable aspects, which can be applied to every application that comes under testing.

Some of the areas check list must cover are:

- Application load time
- Battery behavior
- Airplane mode behavior
- Camera
- Wi-Fi / Bluetooth interruptions
- Sleep mode
- Lock screen
- Device gestures

Expanding on similar lines, one can see that a number of cases can be prepared which can be commonly applied to the application under testing. Every practical scenario in which the mobile device under testing is utilized must be considered and non-functional checklists must be prepared to cover all these cases. Usability and accessibility, which includes the font and font sizes, must top the list of the checklist points. Display methods, input options, common touch points and general keys must be considered and scenarios must be built to cover them in the non-functional checklist.

This type of a non-functional round of testing would help us save a lot of time while executing actual application specific tests. In fact, non-functional checklist test execution must be a mandatory part of test cycles to ensure proper working of the device. The best approach would be to create a checklist with all possible nonfunctional scenarios covered and then share it with the team. The team must then choose the applicable checkpoints from the list and execute them to ensure proper coverage.

Functional: this is the most important part of this book. Approaching the actual mobile application testing. Functional testing is all about understanding the behavior of the application on the mobile device. Confirming that requirements are implemented and working as expected. Functional testing of a mobile application is unlike carrying out functional testing on a web application or a desktop application. In the case of a web application or a desktop application Testers need to concentrate a large chunk of testing on the application itself. But in the case of a mobile application it is a different story. There are a number of major parameters that have to be considered:

- Application based
- Device based
- Interruptions based
- Network based
- Security based

Each of these parameters needs to be given priority while approaching mobile application. Hence each of these parameters needs detailed scrutiny and the testing must accommodate all of them. Let us now analyze each of these parameters in detail.

Application based: Functional testing is always application requirements based. An application is built from requirements. Once the build is ready, testing is carried out to ensure the application satisfies all the requirements listed. So let us concentrate on prioritizing application based functional testing and list the check points that must be considered.

o Installation / Uninstallation /updates – First, it is important to test the application installation methods. Users can install the application in a number of ways. Over the Air (OTA), through an application management system MDM or MAM, over cable etc. All the supported types of installation must be tested. It is also important to include testing uninstallation. Testers must ensure that removing an application removes all the associated files and that removal does not in any away affect the working of other applications or the device. It is also important to ensure that no files are left in the device anywhere which can be accessed by other applications. What happens when a new updated version of the existing application is pushed to production? How does the device and functions of the application behave after updates? Does the saved data get lost or become unreadable with the updated version? These are some of the questions that must be answered by carrying out application update tests. It is also important to track the application even at the testing phase, using versions, so that Testers get to test all the possible actions under this heading.

o Functionality – As discussed already, functional testing is the primary type of testing to ensure the application output is as expected. All the requirements must be cross checked to ensure that they match the requirements that were drafted and agreed. This is a critical check point. For a mobile application there are many associated check points that ensure the application works perfectly:

o UX (User Experience) – First impressions do matter. And User experience is the key player in forming impressions. A study conducted back in 2011 (when the number of mobile applications available was approximately 1/8th of what it is today!) shows that 26% of the applications downloaded are deleted immediately after the first use. One of the major reasons why users tend to abandon them is poor user experience. As a Tester it is important to scan each screen / module and check the fonts, sizes, placement of images, color combinations and visual appearance. If any of them are noted as sub-standard it must immediately pushed back to the development team to avoid making your application a failure in production.

o Touch points – Touch points are the areas on the screen that trigger a response to the user when touched. Touch points contribute to the user experience. It is important to know the placement of buttons, textboxes, checkboxes or even dropdowns in applications. Users must be able to reach the touch points with ease. Care must be taken to ensure proper space is provided between each touch point to avoid unexpected output. Extra testing must be put in place for touch point placement in gaming apps, as even the slightest unexpected result can disappoint the user and result in discarding the application.

o Crashes – One of the catastrophic results of a buggy application is crashing. Crashing can at times even end up requiring rebooting of the phone and sometimes make the device hang. Users do not expect an application to provide them with a damaged operating system which forces them to restart their device. Hence it is very important that Testers cover all possible test cases to ensure that application crashes are detected at any point of an application's use. Test cases that require the application to pull down large amounts of data or push large amounts of data to the servers must be double checked to ensure it works as expected without any crashes or hanging.

o Memory Management –Smart phones have very good hardware specs in place these days, which also includes high speed processers and plentiful RAM. And unlike earlier days of mobile apps, the application development platforms also have very good memory management system in place which helps developers fine tune heavy pieces of code to manage the memory well. The iOS application development platform Xcode has ARC

(Automatic Reference Counting) which helps the developer to a great extent in managing the memory efficiently. Such systems are in place for other development platforms too. As a Tester, it is important to check for all the modules that involve heavy memory usage so as to understand potential performance issues that must be reported to the developers as soon as detected. Due to advanced technology, it is easy to fix these memory related defects these days.

- o Screen Orientation – Screen orientation is an integral aspect of mobile devices which impacts on several parameters that Testers consider while testing mobile applications. Native applications can be orientation blocked. That is, it can be restricted to either work only in landscape mode or portrait mode. Hence the Tester must take care to ensure that the orientation limitations are obeyed. Also for web applications where orientation cannot be controlled, Testers must ensure they carry out all the test cases in both modes and ensure proper operation. From experience, it is noted that an application's look and feel gets distorted when orientation changes. The most common defects noted with applications that support both orientations are links not working, images not loading properly, pixilated images or even missing buttons or input boxes. Hence it is very important for the Tester to ensure that the application works perfectly as expected in whichever mode the user uses it.

- o Performance – Performance of an application has many attributes and needs a very detailed study. Detailed discussion on performance testing is covered in the chapter entitled 'Mobile application automation and performance testing'. A simple test cycle that every Tester must execute should be to check the time taken to execute an action. A simple example to check performance of an application would be to use a stop watch to check the time taken to load the application main menu from the time the user presses the login button. Every such action must be noted and a tabular record should be maintained right from the first version of the application build to ensure that all performance changes are tracked and marked.

- o Process time – Process time is an attribute of the performance just discussed above. Let us try to analyze why it is important to discuss this feature in detail. How many of us have seen websites that show a blank screen for more than 5 seconds before loading? It is a common tendency to hit the refresh button when the screen stays blank for more than three seconds. So process time matters a lot when it comes to providing a satisfactory experience to the user. Hence it is important to address these blank spots no matter which type of mobile application is under testing. Any action within the application that takes more than three or four seconds must be accompanied by an activity indicator to let the user know that some action is taking place in the background. Hence process times require special attention to ensure that user engagement is established with the application all the time.

Device based: -Functional testing of mobile applications needs a greater deal of attention from the perspective of device behavior too. It is important to understand device behavior due to the application under test. Most users may discard the application if it in any way affects the performance of the device. Some statistics from 2013 mention that every 5 minutes, 3 applications are added to Google Play alone. Alternative applications are available with just one press of a button these days. Hence utmost priority must be given to ensuring that the application under test does not affect the overall performance of the device in any way. Normal performance of the device must be ensured in all possible scenarios with the application. Device perspective of functional testing has a greater significance for native and hybrid applications than web applications. Therefore, while testing native or hybrid applications, one must make sure to check all possible aspects that affect the device. Below are a few important parameters from the device perspective that must be considered while executing tests:

o Operating Systems – The first point of consideration from the device perspective would be to understand the operating systems on which the application is expected to work. Testers must ensure they execute the application on each of the intended operating systems if possible on the real device. A major point to check here would be to understand the interaction of the application with the operating systems and also to list any exceptions thrown by the application due to any compatibility issues it has with the operating system on which it is working.

o **Versions** – Another important aspect to be considered for mobile applications are the versions of the operating system it must support. As the operating system owners send out updates very regularly with many new features, there are a number of things that Testers must add to their 'to do' list while preparing to test a mobile application. One of them is to work with the application owners and identify the number of versions of the operating systems the application must support. In the first chapter of this book, operating systems and versions are discussed in detail and this helps in understanding the need for narrowing down the operating system versions for mobile application testing. The second approach would be also to prepare a set of test cases that must be executed every time the operating system owners introduce a new version into the market. This will help to understand the tweaks needed to the application to make it work without any showstoppers on the new version of the operating systems. It is also good to read in detail the release notes of the new version to understand the major changes they have carried out on the operating systems so that further fine tuning of test cases can be carried out to ensure that application is not in any way affected by the changes on the operating system.

o **Camera** – A mobile phone is a combination of a number of everyday gadgets. Some of them are the camera, GPS and even the accelerometer. Each of these gadgets present in the mobile either helps the application or act independently to support the user. Hence it is important that Testers concentrate on each of them and design test cases to confirm the application does not in any away affect the proper working of these built in features of the device. Tests must also be designed to cover the reverse approach, which is to ensure that once the user returns to the application after using the camera, the application under test works as expected. Two check points under this section would be to ensure that interaction between camera and application (if the camera is used from within the application) is done without any noticeable delays or defects. The other point is to check it is working independently. Use the application to switch to camera and capture a video or an image and come back to check how the application behaves. These tests may sometimes appear silly but there are many instances when a device has struggled to recover from defects highlighted by these types of tests.

- GPS – Global Positioning System is yet another very important and popular inbuilt tool. Even though users don't notice it, there are many features that GPS in the mobile can help with. Roughly more than 50% of mobile applications at one point or other utilize GPS to provide users with better facilities, be it advertisements or offers or exact location or even tracking friends and relatives who are close by. Battery consumption rate is an important tracking parameter while testing an application that uses GPS. It is a well-known fact that GPS is one of the most battery draining applications. Hence extra care should be taken while working with applications that have GPS integrated to ensure that they pull data only when needed rather than keeping it active all the time which may affect the battery life of the mobile and will disappoint the user. It is very important to identify all the areas within the application that drain the battery and reduce them to a controllable level.

- Accelerometer – This is a tool that can sense the orientation of the device, measure magnitude, acceleration and speed. Knowingly or unknowingly, every user who uses mobile utilizes the inbuilt accelerometer. The moment the device is rotated while reading a web page, the web page also changes its orientation to match the action performed. Have you ever wondered how it is achieved? It is the accelerometer that does the magic. The accelerometer is a very important factor of a mobile application. Some mobile applications use this accelerometer extensively. The best example would be the need for speed games or Angry Birds. It is not just games that use them but almost any application that needs to identify the magnitude, acceleration or speed of the device. Design test cases to incorporate all the areas of the application where accelerometers are used and all possible results must be captured to confirm it is working as intended. To understand them in detail, it is also advised to learn in depth the outputs that the accelerometer provides and how the application uses them from the designers.

o Screen size & Resolutions – Yet another point that is already mentioned in chapter one. Testing must cover most popular device sizes and resolutions. Screen size and resolution changes can at times affect the visual appeal of the application and end up missing some important pieces of the display on the screen. Hence build test cases to ensure both UI and functionality work the same for all types. This is to ensure that the application works perfectly on all devices and the device is not affected when navigating away or within the application.

o Notifications – From a device perspective, notifications play a major role whether it is from the application under testing or from any other application installed on the device. Notifications can be from the device such as battery related, network changes etc. They can also be from other applications like Facebook, alarm, calendar etc. Testers must accommodate such notification test cases and ensure the device behaves correctly.

o Power – Another device aspect that needs special attention are the variations to be noticed with power factors. There are a number of items to be added to the 'to do' list of Testers while preparing test cases for this characteristic. One is to check the overall battery drainage while using the application. Another would be to check the working of the application while the device is charging, and another would be to test the application under low battery and work with it till the battery goes dead. It must be confirmed that the device reboots normally once the battery is charged up again. At times it is noted that when the phone goes off while working with an application, it generates undesired results when restarted. There are many reasons that contribute to this. Hence, as a Tester, care must be taken to ensure that our device is not impacted by the application. Battery change notifications must also be considered and tested to ensure the application continues to work as expected even if the notifications come up unexpectedly.

Interruptions based: Another mobile platform specific characteristic would be interruptions. Interruptions are unexpected events that can happen at any point. Hence it is necessary to draft test cases for all types of interruption that can occur on the device. Let us now try to list the types of interruptions that take place on a mobile device:

o   Calls – Incoming calls and outgoing calls must be added as a test case to the existing application's test cases to see how the application behaves on returning from the action. Data transfers, video streaming, time bound games all need to be checked for behavior on interruption from incoming or outgoing calls. The desired actions in case of an interruption must be discussed and drafted out so that Testers can create test cases to ensure all these scenarios are covered in testing.

o   SMS / MMS – SMS or MMS reach the device as a notification but most of the latest smartphones have the capacity these days to display the message right away. Hence while using the application under test it is important to mimic the SMS or MMS incoming scenarios so as to understand how the keyboards and other associated resource behave in response to this quick change. Also it is important to check how the application executes when any incoming or outgoing MMS or SMS are triggered from or to the mobile device.

o   Alerts / Notifications – Interruptions happen in the case of alerts too, such as installed application specific, alarms, calendar etc. It is always good to have the most common applications installed on the test device, like Twitter, Facebook, share notifications systems or any chat applications to see the effect of notifications from these applications while working with the application under test. Test cases must be created considering all these scenarios. It is important to have interruptions triggered at a time when the application under test is either receiving data from the server or sending data to the server to get better results.

o   Power – Power variations in the device pushes many alerts. Alerts in connection with attaching a charger, Battery full, Battery low, Charger removal alert etc. Test cases must address all these interruptions triggered from a power cycle point of view. Application behavior must be noted and any undesired output must be tracked to closure.

o   Data Transfers (Wired / Wireless) – Interruptions do happen when the device is connected to a computer using a USB cable or even to another device using Bluetooth. USB cable data transfer connection or a file being sent from a Bluetooth paired device can trigger a confirmation alert to the user. Such alerts need to be tracked over a test case. Application continuity must be ensured even in the occurrence of such alerts.

o   Media Player – Interruption from a media player to the application under test can happen when trying to open a video or audio file from within the application. Testers must take note of the behavior of the application once the action is completed by the video. The application must resume working normally as soon as the video player moves away. Any alerts from the video player also must be marked. It is important that the application continues to communicate properly with the media player and resumes its normal operation without causing any interference to the device.

Network based: Mobile devices depend a lot on the network being active and executing the requested actions. Smartphones can be connected to the Internet using the carrier network or using Wi-Fi. Testers must have a clear understanding of the networks that the application must work smoothly with. Once the network details are available the following check points must be considered to build a fool proof test cases.

o Over Carrier Network – Internet access provided through the sim card available on the smartphones is considered as carrier network. It helps to understand the different carrier networks and the advances in them:

Abbreviation	Expansion	Specifications
GPRS	General Packet Radio Service	2G Technology Download speed up to 114Kbps Data cannot be sent when a voice call is in progress
EDGE	Enhanced Data GSM Evolution	2G Technology Download speed up to 384Kbps Sometimes also known as 2.5G network
2G	2nd Generation Wireless Communication Technology	Launched in 1991 Technology is GSM (Global System for Mobile communication) based uses TDMA (Time Division Multiple Access) or CDMA (Time Division Multiple Access)
3G	3rd Generation Wireless Communication Technology	Launched in 2001 Download speed up to 3.1 Mbps Technology is ITU (International Telecommunication Union) Supports video calls Supports CDMA, TDMA and FDMA technologies
HSDPA	High-Speed Down-link Packet Access	Based on 3G network Download speed can be up to 14Mbps At times also called as 3.5G
4G	4th Generation Wireless Communication Technology	Launched in 2008 Based on all-IP packet switched network Data rates up to 100Mbit/s Smooth handovers across heterogeneous networks High quality service with next generation multimedia support.
HSPA+	Evolved High-Speed Packet Access	4G Technology Download Speed up to 168Mbps

		4G Technology
4G LTE	4th Generation Long Term Evolution	Download Speed up to 299.6Mbps Supports HD video streaming

The application under test must be run through all possible mobile networks and it is always advisable to carry out this network specific testing on real devices.

o　　Wi-Fi – Another option for smartphones to get connected to the network is using Wi-Fi. Smartphones depend a lot on these types of wireless connections as they have higher speed. Commercially, Wi-Fi started to be in use from 2000 and since then the quality and speed of this connection type has been on the rise. These days there are no applications that do not support Wi-Fi connections. Some enterprise applications work only on specific Wi-Fi connection or through VPN (Virtual Private Network). Hence such applications must be tested with VPN and without VPN to ensure proper information in the form of an alert is passed to the user when they are trying to connect using any unidentified Wi-Fi connections.

o　　Network Interoperability – Network transition or interoperability is yet another interesting test that has to be carried out on mobile applications. Interoperability testing is nothing other than the behavior of the application when the network is changed from one to another. Some of the most popular interoperability testing is done for Wi-Fi to 3G, 3G to 2G, 2G to 3G and 3G to Wi-Fi. All mobile network carrier interoperability testing is easy to execute as the device has options within its settings menu to set they type of mobile network it must access. Testers need to change them and check the behavior of the application. The most frequently required network interoperability testing is between Wi-Fi and mobile network. Most users have the tendency to use Wi-Fi wherever available and walk away continuing to be connected to Internet using mobile network. Hence it is important for Testers to ensure that all the mobile applications are put through these tests to ensure proper operation during transitions. One of the easiest methods to tackle transition testing is by connecting the device to a

Wi-Fi connection and start using the mobile application. Now while using the application start to walk away from the router providing the Wi-Fi until it is out of range and the device connects to the Internet automatically using mobile carrier. Study and record the changes noticed and confirm that the application behaves as expected. Walking into a trusted Wi-Fi connection from a mobile network must also be executed to ensure the proper operation of the application.

- Network Fluctuations – Weak network always tend to cause trouble for mobile applications. Hence Testers must also be familiar with tackling such situations. When data transfer takes place between the application and server over a weak network, the failure rates are high. How equipped or how elegantly the application handles such failures should be assessed. Does it provide correct information back to the user or end up crashing the application? Now the question arises on how to create network fluctuations. As mentioned previously it is always advisable to have the network related tests carried out on real devices only, to get the best results. Hence it is important to create the fluctuations on a real device.

  There are a couple of practical methods to recreate this. One way is to start working on the application from outside a building where the network is strong and then walk down to the basement where the network availability is restricted. Another option would be to test in a lift of the building where most often network fluctuations are normal.

- No Network / Airplane Mode –Airplane mode is an option available on smartphones which, once activated, turns off the cellular connection, Wi-Fi, FM radio, and Bluetooth on the phone simultaneously so that user can continue to work with other applications. It is very important to test applications in Airplane mode to check if the right responses are obtained from the application regarding the unavailability of network rather than hanging or crashing the device.

Security: OWASP - The Open Web Application Security Project - Is a not-for-profit charitable organization that aims to provide unbiased, practical, cost-effective information about application security. OWASAP has identified the top 10 mobile security related risks and these are the updates released for 2014:

- o **M1: Weak Server Side Controls** – Some of the reasons for this risk are outsourced code, poor budgets allocated for enhancing mobile security and, most importantly, non-standard cross platform development and compilation.

  One method to avoid this risk is to have a robust process in place for development of mobile applications and follow secure coding and configuration practices to be used on the server side.

  Tester must be equipped to carry out white box testing of all the services shared by the mobile application to ensure that the agreed process is followed while coding. Developers must be encouraged to carry out peer reviews to confirm the adoption of the agreed process. Tests also must check for any web service or API used in the mobile application for data leakage or exploitation.

- o **M2: Insecure Data Storage** – There are a number of instances on mobile devices where applications tend to store data in an insecure manner. Some of them are SQLite databases, Log Files, Plist Files, XML Data Stores or Manifest Files, Binary data stores, Cookie stores, SD Card and Cloud synced.

  Tests must ensure that the application does not store any data on the device unless and until it is absolutely necessary. Also must ensure that proper encryption is in place for sensitive information handled within the application.

o M3: Insufficient Transport Layer Protection – This risk arises when connections are not properly encrypted or properly signed SSL certificates are not used in the application.

A white box testing approach here will help us identify any deviation from the required standards. All connections must be through secured channels which are properly signed by a trusted CA provider.

o M4: Unintended Data Leakage – This can happen when data from the application is saved in a location which can be accessed by other applications installed on the same device. Cached data, images, key presses, logging and buffers are the vulnerable part of the application at risk.

A detailed test must be carried out across the application to ensure that no sensitive data from within the application is placed in common locations that are accessible to other applications. Until and unless absolutely necessary, no data must be cached and check that it is cleared down as soon as the session ends. Cookies of web applications also must be scrutinized during testing to ensure they are not allowed to be accessed by any other applications.

o M5: Poor Authorization and Authentication – Authentication is allowing access to a particular application to a user with approved credentials which, in most cases with mobile applications, would be user name and password. So authentication is nothing but checking for validity of a user. Authorization is the next step in the process, it is all about permissions. The activities that the authenticated user is authorized to do are determined in this section.

In the case of mobile applications, username and password must not be stored locally even if the user selects the 'remember me' option at the login screen. Also check for proper end to end encryption of user name and password. Both authentication and authorization must be checked and approved only at the server side. If the application supports offline authentication and authorization, then all the local integrity checks must be carried out to ensure the credentials are safely maintained.

o   M6: Broken Cryptography – Broken cryptography can result in the unauthorized retrieval of sensitive information from the mobile device. Flawed or weak encryption / decryption methods are the most common reasons found in mobile applications for broken cryptography.

Tests must be carried out to ensure no keys embedded in the application are mishandled. It is also advisable to create and use custom made encryption protocols to ensure strong security is in place for the application under test. And detailed tests must be executed to ensure the APIs and custom made protocols are of high standards.

o   M7: Client Side Injection – Client side injection happens when a malicious code is executed on the mobile device via a mobile application. SQL Injection and Local File Inclusion are two different risks associated with this vulnerability. Java script injection is also possible through mobile browsers.

Tests scenarios must be created to tackle all the above mentioned cases and applications must be subject to rigorous testing to ensure no such injection affects the application.

o   M8: Security Decisions Via Untrusted Inputs – If the application under test requires to communicate with any other sources it is always advisable that a strong Inter Process Communication (IPC) mechanism is applied and that access is allowed only to a white list of trusted applications.

Testing must cover all the interactions the application makes with other sources and must validate the mechanism of communication. Standard IPC protocols must be verified and care must be taken to secure the application.

o   M9: Improper Session Handling - For successful authentication of Sessions in mobile applications, a session cookie is issued from the server and this cookie is added to all the service transactions by the mobile application to fetch data from the server or to insert data into the server. Improper session handling occurs when this session token is shared by mistake with the adversary during these communications between the mobile application and backend server. Some other reasons that add to this risk are lack of adequate session time out protection, failure to properly rotate cookies and insecure token creation.

In order to eliminate these risks, test cases must be created to check the session timeouts and idle timeout of the application to check the auto timeout checks. Also, ensure that proper new cookie creation occurs for every new authentication. In addition, proper destruction of the cookies must be ensured on completion of the session.

- **M10: Lack of Binary Protections** – Binary protection of an application is to ensure that the final build of the application cannot be reverse engineered to expose the underlying code base so that it can be modified to add malware to rebuild. The application also must be protected from recreating the control flow or the pseudo code using any automation tools. Binary protection also protects the application's presentation layer thus avoiding the execution of any modified Java scripts.

Application code must be thoroughly checked to ensure that proper secure coding techniques for security components such as Jailbreak Detection Controls, Checksum Controls, Certificate Pinning Controls and Debugger Detection Controls are in place. The application must be checked to ensure that any code integrity violation is appropriately addressed.

6 Mobile application automation and Performance testing

In this chapter, automation and performance specific testing methods will be discussed in detail. Both automation and performance testing support tools are available in the market and many methods are followed to achieve automation and performance testing. Some of the most commonly used methods and currently trending tools will be analyzed. Many of the latest tools allow the user to automate and carry out performance testing on simulators, cloud devices and real devices. Most tools also mention the support of 'one script, multiple device' method. In short, this allows you to create the script using one device and run the same script on many other devices. That is, one can automate the application using an iOS phone and reuse the same script to run on Android or Windows smartphones.

From practical experience it has been found that many times the 'one script many device options' do not work as expected. Automation specialists have again and again failed to get the right script that works on all devices for the same application. But due to many factors and limitations of the scripting tool it is indeed a very tedious task to build one script for all devices.

In the chapter entitled 'Type of mobile applications', the initial homework one must do to decide on choosing automation of a mobile application has been addressed. In this chapter, techniques used for mobile automation will be elaborated on. From practical experience it has been noticed that even though there are a number of software tools available out there for mobile application automation, mastering them is easy once the common techniques used are understood.

Automation - Common Techniques

There are mainly three common methods by which automation of mobile application can be achieved. They are:
- Record and Play
- Object identification method
- Visual Analysis

Record and Play – Just like any other web or desktop application automation tools, all mobile automation tools also support record and play functionality. The major advantage of this method is that it can be used with both simulator and real devices. This method of automation does not require any in depth technical skills for the recording and execution of the test cases. It is found to be effective on device or simulator. This type of automation is also called macro level automation since capturing or automation of the screen is done without detailed understanding of the actual functionalities of the screen. This type of automation also is not susceptible to defects from the system level as the system just repeats a simple sequence of actions which was previously captured from the same screen.

There are a number of disadvantages to this type of approach. Most of them are the same as those found while carrying out record and play automation in web or desktop systems. Record and play does not actually tell the user what is happening during execution. The user does not have any clue of the test cases covered. The scripts are almost impossible to maintain. Every recording scenario creates a new set of scripts.

Hence fine tuning or maintenance of the script is almost impossible when it comes to record and play. Also any minor change in the application leads to the recapturing of the entire script. There is no way to modify the code to accommodate the new changes.

In short, for any mobile application Record and Play method of automation must be least used or, even better, avoided completely.

Object identification method – The native object identification method is one of the latest and most accurate automation methods added to mobile automation tools. These days most of the mobile automation tools that are introduced to the market adapt to this object identification method.

To give you a simple example, consider a mobile application with a login screen. Let us try to automate the login screen. In the case of record and play, the record button of the automation tool is pressed, followed by entering user name and password and then the login button. This creates the script with the data that was just submitted and then replays. But in the case of object identification, the automation specialists can identify the objects on the login screen such as the labels, textboxes and buttons. This allows creating clearer scripts, to which parameters such as user names and passwords can be passed easily.

There are many advantages of object identification. It allows the creation of less fragile, clearer scripts. Even if the objects are moved, the script will still be able to work as expected. It also gives 100% accurate output unlike the record and play method. Object identification is also supported by most languages. It is also found that this type of approach is faster than the other two methods and gives output quickly. Object identification also supports flexible identification. Flexible identification is about marking the relation between two objects. Relation can be marked between a label and text box, text box and a button or a label and a button etc.

A small example may help to understand this. Let us once again consider the login screen. Let us say the automation tool is able to identify the label 'User Name' but not the text box next to it. In this case, it can be scripted in such a manner that the system will identify the label 'User Name' and place the cursor say to the left by 40 pixels (or any similar parameter), which in fact will place the cursor right inside the user name text box, thus enabling us to input the desired value into the text box.

Even though object identification is widely used these days for mobile automation, this method is also not that perfect. It has many drawbacks. Let us try to summarize the disadvantages:

1. Object identification based automation does not support identification of GUI defects such as truncation of text on the screen or end user experience defects.
2. Not suitable for gaming applications as they are mostly unstructured from a visual point of view
3. Object identification can work only if the browser / application / OS support the exposure of objects.

4. Object identification supports only text from a running application, hence cannot be used for automating an application that has text embedded in an image.
5. Again, objects can be identified only from within the exposed application, hence any alerts triggered from outside the application such as incoming call or SMS or email or any other device triggered notifications won't be accessible using this method.

These limitations actually forced the tool creators to build another method which would cover all the mentioned disadvantages.

Visual Analysis / Optical Character Recognition (OCR) – This method is the latest approach applied specifically for mobile applications automation. To a large extent it supports cover for all the disadvantages of normal object identification methods.

OCR utilizes smart software that compares a stored image from a repository with that on the screen and executes actions as directed. Since image comparison is the main action that takes place, this method is capable of handling images, text or even hand written screens.

Advantages of this method include helping the user identify glitches with end user experience and GUI defects associated with the mobile application under testing. This method implements WYSIWYG (What You See Is What You Get) which actually helps in scripting to evaluate the application for detailed analysis. It does not require applications to expose the objects as it depends on the visual screen.

Yet again this method also has its own disadvantages. Some of them that need attention are:

1. It is not supported by all languages.
2. Since image scanning and comparison is the basis on which this method works, it is slower when compared to object level analysis.
3. OCR works with the help of third party software; this actually increases the expense of automating the mobile application.

Considering the above methods it can be concluded that automation can be made more robust, effective and efficient by considering an intelligent combination of all three methods. This combination helps the user to have greater test case coverage and also to cover UI related test cases. These types of a combination approach help build one script for all devices and promise better results.

Performance and Load testing options

Another most important factor that needs attention in the case of a mobile application is its performance. The performance factors that a common user expects while working on an application are already discussed in the chapter entitled 'Actual mobile test execution'. In addition, it is good to delve deeper into technical aspects of the application development and testing that must be covered under performance and load testing. Let us also try to identify the specific areas that must be considered in the mobile applications test chain for covering end to end mobile application performance fine tuning. There follows a list of important points that one must consider at the time of development and also methods to be followed during testing to ensure they are well within the allowed limits:

Controlling the Memory Leaks – While approaching performance tuning of a mobile application one of the important factors from the device side that must be considered is the memory usage of the application. Vital checks include ensuring the application is not holding or caching data that is not necessary, or not clearing the temporary memory on application exit etc. As all of us are aware, unlike a web application where one can load hundreds of rows of data at a time, on a mobile device this number is drastically reduced as the user also will find difficulty in navigating through this large chunk of data even if the application is capable of handling it. Hence pagination or load on scroll down methods must be in place and must perform well by loading data quickly.

Memory leaks were a major headache for developers who worked with the first generation smartphones and tablets whose physical memory was very limited. But these days with advances in technology and smaller, smarter components, smartphones have better hardware configurations which have reduced the difficulty for developers to write code that performs well. However it is always good to carry out detailed white box testing of the application under test to understand the correct use of loops, data transfer load, data handling method on the device and internal memory usage.

These types of checks can further help reduce memory usage and thus result in improved performance of the application. Checking for memory leaks must start with carrying out those complicated test cases which involve huge data handling or manipulations. If the performance is observed to be unsatisfactory, white box testing of that particular module must be carried out to see if the improvement must be made on the application code or on the services that are called to manage or transfer data to and from the server.

This type of a detailed analysis on the initial build of the application helps both developers and Testers save a large amount of time in the later stages. Hence it is always advised to have detailed code level testing carried out in the very initial stages.

Adhering to CPU limits –The reader may be confused as to what is the difference between this point and the one just discussed above. Adhering to CPU limits greatly helps in containing memory leakages. But along with memory leakages, there are also a number of other situations where the application can test the limits of the CPU of the device it functions on.

To explain one such scenario, consider an application with a module that has a complex calculation in place. Imagine that the application takes data from the user and, based on the data received, it pulls some data from the server if online. Otherwise it takes values from the offline storage system and does the calculation to output the results. Now if this calculation manipulates data from different sources and makes extreme use of all the available resources of the device, it is natural that the CPU usage may go up beyond what the device can handle, resulting in extreme behaviors such as device restart or application crashing.

This is just one scenario where the CPU limits are put to the test and most often it is seen that gaming applications are the ones which test the device CPU to the maximum possible. Hence special attention must be given to such applications.

Here also the best testing approach would be to identify the test scenarios that make the processor work beyond an expected margin. Once these scenarios are identified, prioritize them to be included in the initial round of testing. Results must be analyzed and any irregular behavior must be taken for detailed analysis at the code level and must be modified if necessary.

Network / Bandwidth – Consider the case of a mobile application which replicates an online admission request form, such as provided by a college on their website. Candidates have to supply a great deal of personal, family and academic details to complete the submission. In the case of a website, the complete details are collected on a single page. The data entered is submitted to the server as soon as the user presses the submit button. Would it be a good idea to have the same submission page presented on the mobile application too?

These days the Internet speed on mobile devices has risen in an exponential manner. However there are many other factors that still act as a hindrance to providing a steady network signal strength to the device. Now keeping this factor in mind, it is easy to answer the above question. It is a simple straight forward 'NO'. Performance of an application comes not just from the memory or server or CPU level. It also comes from the network component. Hence it is very important to ensure data transfer over mobile networks is short and fast. Also only the requested data should be handled in this traffic. So then what would be the best approach for the admission form on a mobile application? The best solution would be to break it down into smaller blocks. Categorize the submission forms into personal details, family details, academic details etc. The user must be presented with only one section at a time and on completion of each section, a Next button must be enabled, pressing on which the application must save the data entered and must also load the next section.

Hence it is very important that all such scenarios which require the application to interact with server over a network be considered for criticality and the amount of data transferred. Any heavy traffic observed must be put to rigorous and different network testing. All the points to be considered for network testing have already been addressed in the previous chapter.

Power consumption – One of the performance deciding factors of a mobile application is the power consumption rate. For any user, one of the first noticeable points about a smart phone will be the battery usage. Any user, even those with no technical background, notices their phones battery drainage. No user will risk using an application which consumes the device battery beyond a permissible limit.

It is often found that applications that use GPS are heavy on battery consumption. Some other factors that affect the battery drainage are camera, gyro meter, video player and recording of audio or video etc. If an application uses any of these, then special attention must be given to those test cases. Execution results must be analyzed and recorded. These recorded results must be compared with any stated standards or similar applications to check the difference in consumption. Actions that consume battery power beyond a limit must be notified to the developers and code cleaning should be carried out to lower these readings.

Now that the major parameters that must be attended to in order to increase the performance of an application have been explained, let us now put in place the major components and detailed approach listed to tackle each sector:

Component	What to Test	How	Tools
Server	Source of Request Number of Users Location from where requests are made	Crowd Source Testing Simulation of Load using Tools	HP Load Runner Neo Load SOASTA Cloud Test
Network	Type of Network Load on Network Mobile Network Provider	Real Networks Network Emulation	Shunra Gomez Device Anywhere
Device	OS Type Device Type Browser Type	Real Devices Devices in Cloud Device Emulation	Keynote Web Perspective Device Lab Device Anywhere Perfecto Mobile Gomez
Performance Monitoring	Server Network Device Transaction	Server Monitoring Network Monitoring Response Time/Throughput	HP Site Scope Network Monitoring Solution Instruments DDMS

As stated in the above table, performance tuning is not just restricted to what is installed on the smartphone; there are many other factors that play an important role in getting the performance to the required standards.

Currently trending automation tools

Perfecto	http://www.perfectomobile.com/
Device anywhere	http://www.keynote.com/solutions/testing/mobile-testing
SeeTest	http://experitest.com/
Sikuli	http://www.sikuli.org/
EggPlant	http://www.testplant.com/eggplant/testing-tools/eggplant-mobile-eggon/

Performance tool support for Mobile OS – Performance testing on applications can be carried out from within the development SDK. This actually helps the developers to identify performance related issues right at the beginning. Some of the built in tools are listed below:

Operating System	Tool Details
iOS	Xcode has tools such as Instruments, Shark, activity monitor and bigTop
android	Android Developer Tools (ADT) has profiler tool. HPROF is another powerful tool
BlackBerry	BlackBerry JDE has an inbuilt profile tool which helps in very detailed analysis
Windows	Visual Studio is equipped with Windows Phone Application Analysis tool

- Open source automation tools

Most cloud providers have established integration between the most popular automation tools. One example to point out would be MobileCloud from Perfecto. MobileCloud for HP's Unified Functional Testing (UFT) is one such collaborated product between a cloud provider and an established automation tool provider. Using this MobileCloud, users are allowed to leverage the automation capabilities of Quick Test Professional (QTP) and extend it to the cloud devices provided by Perfecto. This allows the user to create and run test cases from QTP directly on devices provided over cloud by Perfecto.

Another popular open source automation tool is Selenium. Selenium has been also extensively updated and used for mobile application automation. Selendroid and Appium are two open source mobile automation frameworks that are currently gaining popularity, which are derived from Selenium. While Selendriod supports only Android mobile applications testing for native, hybrid and mobile web, Appium supports Android, iOS and Firefox OS which is yet to hit the market. Appium also supports testing of native, hybrid and mobile web. In addition it also supports automation of web applications on desktops.

Both Selendriod and Appium can be used on real devices, simulators and cloud devices.

More details on these tools can be obtained from visiting their sites listed below:

Selendriod : http://selendroid.io/

Appium: http://appium.io/

Some of the leading open source mobile automation tools are listed below:

MonkeyTalk: One of the leading open source mobile automation tools with over 70,000 downloads. It can be used for automation of native, hybrid and mobile web on real devices, cloud devices or on simulators. For more details on this tool visit http://www.cloudmonkeymobile.com/monkeytalk

Robotium: This is an automation tool for Android applications. It has a framework that fully supports native and hybrid applications. https://code.google.com/p/robotium/

For iOS based application automation some of the tools like Zucchini (http://www.zucchiniframework.org/), Calabash (http://calaba.sh/) or KIF- Keep It Functional (https://github.com/kif-framework/KIF) can be used.

- Future of Mobile Test Automation

Mobile intrusion into daily life has been phenomenal in the last few years. Mobile applications are here to stay. Hence the opportunities associated with mobile applications are enormous. It is very important to equip ourselves with the latest trends of the industry and also devise test plans to meet the needs of the end user.

Automation of mobile applications testing is also in a rapidly growing phase. Even though it has a number of drawbacks, over time these tools are definitely going to be of help to Testers in reducing manual intervention and also in speeding up releases. One must constantly keep an eye open for any new tools that are introduced and attend demos and webinars to gain knowledge.

Mobile Device Management

As the presence of mobile devices grows, the technology associated with them is also spread wider in a number of ways. Gone are the days when the user used to lose the device and end up worrying about important information stored on the device getting into the wrong hands. These days, by the click of a button on a website, one can locate the device or even format / wipe clean its data. The security of the applications and data stored in the devices are very important and the need to protect them has led to the invention of many software applications. As a Tester, it is always good to have an awareness of these supporting tools and software applications as they sometime communicate or interact with the application under test on the device.

Large enterprises are always on the lookout for ways of improving the service and experience but at a reduced cost. This constant pursuit for better service at reduced price has resulted in companies accommodating new ways to manage their day to day operations more effectively. One of the major changes that are highly visible in such large enterprises is the cost reduction in the area of hardware procurement. Unlike in the past, most companies have very strict rules in place about device purchase. Recently some companies have even stopped purchasing mobile devices. But at the same time there are a number of realistic and employee friendly options available to run the business smoothly. In the first part of this chapter let us get familiar with the device management system that has resulted in increased productivity and collaboration within organizations using available options.

Before the details of the device management options are discussed, it is good to have an understanding of the device environments available to enterprises. The most popular ones are:

- Enterprise supplied Devices
- Bring Your Own Devices (BYOD)
- Bring Your Own Applications (BYOA)

Enterprise supplied Devices

This is the oldest and traditional model of device management supply system followed by enterprises. Most companies depending on employee designation and service expertise, procure devices that are permitted by their security team and supply them for official use. This allowed companies to reap the benefit of providing better services to the customers quickly as they had their employees connected to the company network and its resources all the time. The tradition of supplying devices started with laptops and these days it has become a common practice by companies to provide mobile devices to employees.

But this comes with lot of downside. The cost associated with device procurement and maintenance, along with the running cost of ensuring security compliance, has forced companies to assign large budgets for infrastructure management. Most companies realized that this expense was adversely affecting their profits and devised methods that ensured they spend less on infrastructure. The two methods discussed below are born out of the necessity for companies to find better means of managing their infrastructure cost.

When approaching the testing of a mobile application intended for the internal use of an enterprise, it is very important to have the list of devices approved by the compliance team and the permitted versions of each operating system made available so that better planning of application testing can be done. It is important for the Testers to have access to this data so that estimation and execution of tests are carried out to cover these devices. Other common parameters that need attention in this case are permitted networks, security rules etc.

Bring Your Own Devices (BYOD)

As the title implies, companies allow their employees to bring their own devices to access internal networks and execute their duties. There are several advantages associated with BYOD

- Cost reduction – Lower cost associated with procurement and maintenance
- Better device – Employees usually opt for the latest gadgets in the industry which enables them to execute their activities faster resulting in improved service
- Flexibility and freedom for employees – BOYD provides an opportunity for employees to embrace whichever gadget they feel comfortable to use.
  Improved productivity – Employees tend to spend more time on their own devices and personalized applications which enables them to give a better output.

Now from a mobile application Testers standpoint, applications built for companies adapting BYOD requires extensive ground work. The checklist must contain the company rules for using the application, access rights and access methods. Also, if possible, a list of devices currently used by the employees must be obtained. This will help in creating better test suites to cover most used devices or operating systems. Unlike testing an application that is intended for public use, BYOD intended applications need additional scanning to ensure company they are security complaint and use proper connectivity protocols. The disadvantages of BYOD include lost or stolen devices leading to company data leakage, employee misuse or the potential threat of malware or virus also must be accommodated in the testing suite. Testing must ensure that the application is capable of handling these threats. Avoiding data storage on device, minimal interaction with other resources or applications within the device etc. must be tested for.

Bring Your Own Applications (BYOA)

With companies exploring opportunities to provide better services to customers in a cost effective manner, they have been open to a number of innovative ideas. One of the most popular being BYOA. Taking advantage of millions of free applications available in the market, companies are allowing their employees to bring value add to their business by the effective utilization of these applications. Even though the concept of BYOA is still in its infancy, there are a number of companies utilizing it. As a Tester, this change in environment must be fully understood and the impact to the company must be assessed. Most companies rely a lot on security testing and also data management of these applications that are allowed within their networks. It is a tedious job for the mobile application Tester to cover all aspects of threats arising from BOYA. But with proper planning and detailed test execution, the experience of BYOA can be improved. Testers must be equipped to test any application for vulnerabilities and potential security threats to the network. Creating a well-defined checklist accommodating all the important aspects such as data security, virus threats, communication encryption methods etc. can speed up the process of adding new accepted applications in BYOA thus helping companies to achieve better customer satisfaction.

Enterprise Mobility Management (EMM)

Having covered the main aspects of enterprise approach towards acceptance of mobile and mobile applications, it is also necessary to get familiar with the different methods enterprises adopt to control the interaction of mobile and mobile applications with their networks and also keep track of devices to take appropriate action in the event of theft or loss. One of the primary requirements of a good device management system is to have the ability to manage different operating system loaded devices. There are a number of methods companies depend on to control mobile devices which in a nutshell can be called "Enterprise Mobility Management (EMM)". Some of the leading methods and leaders in the space are discussed below:

- Mobile Device Management (MDM)
- Mobile Application Management (MAM)
- Mobile Information Management (MIM)

Mobile Device Management (MDM)

It is one of the proven and effective methods of managing mobile devices for enterprises. Here the device is fully controlled and monitored by companies. One of the strongest features that attracts most companies to adopt MDM is its capability to manage configurations and enforce policies for regular virus scan and controlled connectivity to virtual private networks.

MDM also allows remote installation of Emails, importing of contacts from corporate addresses, content management and strict control on applications that are installed on the device. Companies also can decide on establishing rules for resetting passwords or PIN's as needed from their own mobile devices. MDM can enforce user specific rules by placing them under specific groups. This helps MDM to provide special privileges to elite groups as needed.

While testing an application that is moderated through MDM, one must replicate the same environment for testing. Applications must be pushed through MDM and confirm that they are working on the device. Also remote wiping of the application must be checked. Once the application is removed from the device, a detailed scan of the device must be carried out to ensure that no data was left in the device by the removed application.

It is always good to be familiar with some of the leading MDM providers in the market to access the advantages of each of them and also to prepare test suites that best match each of the providers:

Providers	Link
AirWatch	http://www.air-watch.com/
Mobileiron	http://www.mobileiron.com/en
AmTel MDM	https://www.amtelnet.com/
XenMobile	http://www.citrix.com/products/xenmobile/overview.html
Boxtone	http://www1.good.com/good-dynamics-platform/boxtone.html

Mobile Application Management (MAM)

As the name suggests, this type of device management concentrates on application level management and not device level. MAM is relatively new when compared to MDM and was born out of the complaints of micro management of devices carried out by MDM which made employees uncomfortable and stopped them from bringing their own devices to work. MAM comes in really handy in case of BYOD enabled companies as it helps in reducing device cost as discussed earlier in this chapter. Users also feel comfortable in adopting MAM in their personal devices as it helps them execute office work right from their own device and they do not have to bother about sharing personal data loaded in the device with device management system. At the same time, companies also get total control over applications that are used to connect to their network or execute activities related to office work. There are a number of features that are supported by MAM. Here are some:

- Delivery of applications from Enterprise App Store

- Force application updating
- Performance monitoring of the application
- Version Management
- Push notification services
- Crash log reporting
- User authorization / authentication
- Reporting and tracking usage analytics

These are some of the major check points that must be accommodated in the test suite of applications that will be catered for using MAM. Most of the leading providers of MDM also have MAM solutions suited to meet the needs of enterprises.

Use these links to get familiar with some of the leading MAM providers:

Providers	Link
Apperian	http://www.apperian.com/
VMWare	http://www.vmware.com/
Workspot inc	http://www.workspot.com/
SOTI	https://www.soti.net/solutions/applicationmanagement/

Mobile Information Management (MIM)

The concept of MIM arose from the thought of unifying the point of contact for accessing sensitive data from an enterprise from all sorts of devices, be they laptops, mobiles or tablets. In this case the all the information needed to be accessed by the employees is encrypted and shared over secure channels to any device, on confirmation that the credentials entered are permitted to access the requested data. Even though at present MIM is under criticism for its disadvantages like incapability of end to end monitoring and inability to exercise end to end control, companies are on the lookout for such solutions which in the near future will reduce their investments on device management solutions to a greater extent.

Rooting / Jail Breaking

Another interesting term one must get familiar with in the mobility space is Rooting or jail breaking. Rooting is a term that refers to Android devices whereas jail breaking is mostly associated with Apple related products. So what exactly does it mean? It is basically the actions performed on the phone to remove certain restrictions put in place by the manufacturers. Users opt to jail break or root their device to gain access to operating folders of the system and to make modifications to the device. This also allows them to install applications that are otherwise restricted by the manufactures as they deem them to be dangerous to the device. Hence jail breaking or rooting is something carried out by the owner of the device without the permission of the manufacturer. This also results in invalidating the warranty provided by these manufacturers.

From a Tester's point of view if an application is intended for public use, it is always good to carry out a round of testing on the jail broken or rooted device to ensure that the data shared from the device cannot be accessed using any other application or is not available in any other folders within the device. This also helps in making the application more secure and less vulnerable to external attacks.

Index

Author

Jeesmon Jacob is an Electronics and Telecommunications engineer with a MBA in IT & Systems. A certified professional in CSTE & ISTQB with over 8 years of experience in the field of Quality Assurance, he is also a Six Sigma green belt certified professional.

With several white papers on mobile application testing, he is a well-established trainer with over 300 hours of successful training under his belt for CMMI practices, Internal Quality Audit Training, Mobile Application Testing, Manual Testing and Best Testing Practices.

Jeesmon has worked as the QA lead for a fortune 500 company and has delivered over 100+ mobile applications on iPhone, iPad, BlackBerry, Android and Windows phones. He is also an expert in mobile test estimating and automation using mobile cloud testing providers such as Perfecto.

Some of his recent works are listed below:

- *Author of white paper " Mobile Apps : Testers' view" (on 25 June 2010).*
- *Presented a white paper entitled "Exploratory Testing for Mobile Apps in Agile SDLC" in the regional qualification round of Software Testing Conference 2010 at Chennai.*
- *Author of the article "Improving the Test Process" in Testing Experience -The magazine for professional testers, with 350,000 downloads and a circulation of 12,000 printed copies per issue.*
- *Co- author of white paper "Roadblocks and their work around while testing Mobile Applications" Published in Testing Experience.*
- *Presented to Mobile Monday (MoMo) Trivandrum community on the topic "Five point mobile testing approach".*